OCEAN LIFE UP CLOSE

Orcas

by Heather Adamson

BLASTOFF! READERS
3

BELLWETHER MEDIA • MINNEAPOLIS, MN

Note to Librarians, Teachers, and Parents:

Blastoff! Readers are carefully developed by literacy experts and combine standards-based content with developmentally appropriate text.

Level 1 provides the most support through repetition of high-frequency words, light text, predictable sentence patterns, and strong visual support.

Level 2 offers early readers a bit more challenge through varied simple sentences, increased text load, and less repetition of high-frequency words.

Level 3 advances early-fluent readers toward fluency through increased text and concept load, less reliance on visuals, longer sentences, and more literary language.

Level 4 builds reading stamina by providing more text per page, increased use of punctuation, greater variation in sentence patterns, and increasingly challenging vocabulary.

Level 5 encourages children to move from "learning to read" to "reading to learn" by providing even more text, varied writing styles, and less familiar topics.

Whichever book is right for your reader, Blastoff! Readers are the perfect books to build confidence and encourage a love of reading that will last a lifetime!

This edition first published in 2018 by Bellwether Media, Inc.

No part of this publication may be reproduced in whole or in part without written permission of the publisher. For information regarding permission, write to Bellwether Media, Inc., Attention: Permissions Department, 5357 Penn Avenue South, Minneapolis, MN 55419.

Library of Congress Cataloging-in-Publication Data

Names: Adamson, Heather, 1974- author.
Title: Orcas / by Heather Adamson.
Description: Minneapolis, MN : Bellwether Media, Inc., [2018] | Series:
    Blastoff! Readers. Ocean Life Up Close | Audience: Ages 5-8. | Audience: K
    to grade 3. | Includes bibliographical references and index.
Identifiers: LCCN 2016052728 (print) | LCCN 2017019062 (ebook) | ISBN
    9781626176430 (hardcover : alk. paper) | ISBN 9781681033730 (ebook)
Subjects: LCSH: Killer whale–Juvenile literature.
Classification: LCC QL737.C432 (ebook) | LCC QL737.C432 A284 2018 (print) |
    DDC 599.53/6–dc23
LC record available at https://lccn.loc.gov/2016052728

Editor: Christina Leighton   Designer: Lois Stanfield

Printed in the United States of America, North Mankato, MN.

Table of Contents

What Are Orcas?

Orcas are fierce, powerful hunters. These **mammals** are very smart.

Other Dolphins

bottlenose dolphins

spinner dolphins

striped dolphins

Orcas are often called killer whales. But they are actually the world's largest dolphins!

Species Spotlight
ORCA

life span:
50 to 80 years

depth range:
0 to 984 feet
(0 to 300 meters)

orca range =

N
W — E
S

conservation status: endangered

| Extinct | Extinct in the Wild | Critically Endangered | Endangered | Vulnerable | Near Threatened | Least Concern |

Orcas swim in all the world's oceans. They are most often found in cold, coastal waters.

They go to the surface to breathe. Each orca has a **blowhole** to take in air. Orcas may also **breach** to breathe. Then they make a noisy splash back into the water!

breaching

blowhole

Big, Black, and White

Orcas are huge. They can be 32 feet (10 meters) long.

Orca Size

orca

average
human

up to 32 feet
(10 meters) long

Males can weigh up to 22,000 pounds (10,000 kilograms). Females are a little smaller.

Identify an Orca

black-and-white skin

tall dorsal fin

large teeth

Orcas have powerful tail fins with two **flukes**. These push the mammals forward.

Orcas steer with side **flippers**. A tall **dorsal fin** keeps orcas balanced.

dorsal fin

flippers

flukes

Orca skin is colored for sneaking up on **prey**. The black looks like water from above. The white looks like the surface from below.

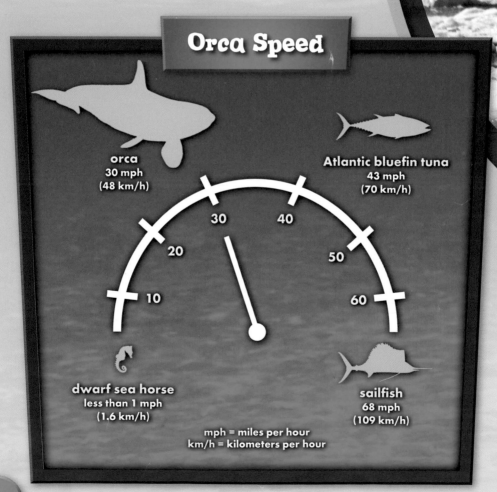

Orca Speed

orca
30 mph
(48 km/h)

Atlantic bluefin tuna
43 mph
(70 km/h)

30   40
20   50
10   60

dwarf sea horse
less than 1 mph
(1.6 km/h)

sailfish
68 mph
(109 km/h)

mph = miles per hour
km/h = kilometers per hour

Beneath their skin, a layer of **blubber** keeps them warm in cold water.

Orcas are often called wolves of the sea.

They live and hunt in groups called **pods**. These can have as many as 40 orcas!

pod

Catch of the Day

Atlantic herring

harbor seals

chinstrap penguins

Orcas eat about 500 pounds (227 kilograms) of food each day.

They slam their bodies against prey. These **carnivores** also make waves to push prey like penguins off floating ice. Some orcas even slide onto shore to grab food!

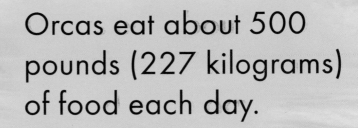

Orcas use sounds to talk to each other underwater. They whistle and call to other orcas. Each pod has its own sounds.

Orcas also make clicking noises for **echolocation**. This helps them find prey and swim without crashing into things.

Female orcas have **calves** every three to ten years. Calves drink milk from their mothers until they learn to hunt.

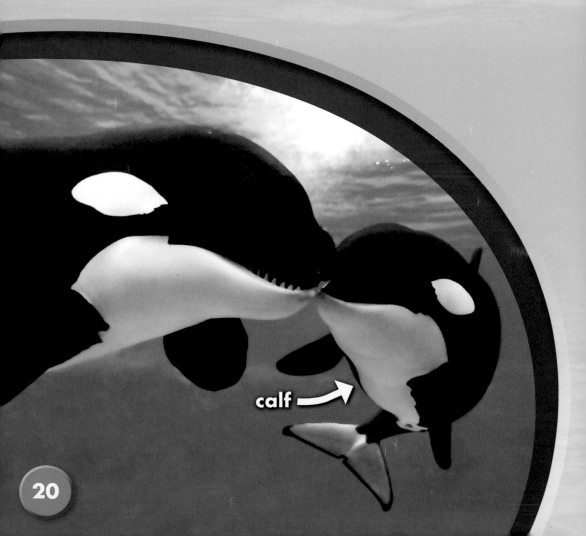

calf →

As adults, orcas do not have **predators**. They rule the ocean!

Glossary

blowhole—the hole on top of an orca's head that is used for breathing

blubber—the fat of orcas

breach—to leap out of the water

calves—baby orcas

carnivores—animals that only eat meat

dorsal fin—the fin on top of an orca's back

echolocation—the use of sound waves and echoes to determine where objects are

flippers—flat, wide body parts that are used for swimming

flukes—the two halves of an orca's tail fin

mammals—warm-blooded animals that have backbones and feed their young milk

pods—groups of orcas

predators—animals that hunt other animals for food

prey—animals that are hunted by other animals for food

To Learn More

AT THE LIBRARY
Allyn, Daisy. *Killer Whales Are Not Whales!* New York, N.Y.: Gareth Stevens Publishing, 2015.

Heos, Bridget. *Do You Really Want to Meet an Orca?* Mankato, Minn.: Amicus High Interest Amicus Ink, 2016.

Zuchora-Walske, Christine. *Killer Whales: Built for the Hunt*. North Mankato, Minn.: Capstone Press, 2016.

ON THE WEB
Learning more about orcas is as easy as 1, 2, 3.

1. Go to www.factsurfer.com.

2. Enter "orcas" into the search box.

3. Click the "Surf" button and you will see a list of related web sites.

With factsurfer.com, finding more information is just a click away.

Index

The images in this book are reproduced through the courtesy of: sakiflower1988, front cover (orca); Dmitry Polonskiy, front cover (background); Rich Carey, pp. 2-3 (background), 22-24; Miles Away Photography, pp. 3 (orca), 6; Arco Images GmbH/ Alamy, pp. 4-5, 8-9, 19, 20, 21; Tory Kallman, p. 5 (top); Anna segeren, p. 5 (center); Gonzalo Jara, p. 5 (bottom); Design Pics Inc/ Alamy, p. 7; sethakan, p. 7 (inset); friedgreenbeans, p. 10 (top right); Mike Price, p. 10 (bottom); Monika Wieland, p. 10 (top center); underworld, p. 10 (top left); Juniors / Juniors/ SuperStock, pp. 10-11; National Geographic Creative/ Alamy, pp. 12-13; Paul Nicklen/ Getty Images, p. 14; Francois Gohier/ VWPics/ Alamy, pp. 14-15, 17; Henrik Larsson, p. 16 (left); Randimal, p. 16 (center); robert mcgillivray, p. 16 (right); WILDLIFE GmbH/ Alamy, pp. 16-17; Nic Hamilton/ Alamy, p. 18.